# THE EFFECTIVE ART OF INFLUENCE PEOPLE

# RAPHAEL DUME

*Copyright © 2019 by Raphael Dume*

*All rights reserved. No part of this publication may be reproduced, distributed, or transmitted in any form or by any means, including photocopying, recording, or other electronic or mechanical methods, without the prior written permission of the publisher, except in the case of brief quotations embodied in critical reviews and certain other noncommercial uses permitted by copyright law.*

**ISBN:** 9781095682272

*Manufactured in the United States of America*

## Contents

Introduction ........................................... 7

Chapter One ......................................... 12

    Getting the right people on your side ......................................................... 12

        Collaborate with like-minded people ........................................... 14

        Getting along with people ......... 16

Chapter two ......................................... 23

    Effective communication .............. 23

    Passion ............................................ 26

    Listen twice, talk once .................. 28

    Be genuinely interested in others' point of view ................................. 31

    Make your team feel important ..... 34

Chapter three ....................................... 38

    Steer clear of arguments ................ 38

    Apologize when you are wrong .... 41

    Be gracious in your correction ...... 43

- Focus only on the present fault .44
- Show your fallibility ................45
- Vital questions to consider before correcting others...........................47
  - Is now the right time for correction?.................................47
  - Am I now in the right frame of mind to correct someone? .........49
  - Can this mistake be overlooked? ................................................51
  - Is this a repeated mistake? ........52
- Chapter four ......................................56
  - How to sell your ideas...................56
    - Identify your market .................58
    - Brand yourself...........................60
    - Know your competitors.............63
    - Build your army ........................66
    - Be an expert: creatively demonstrate your idea...............73
- Chapter five........................................80
  - The science of being influential....80
    - Cause and effect........................81
    - Value .........................................84

- Attraction .................................. 86
- Sacrifice .................................... 88
- Integrity .................................... 90
- Time .......................................... 92

Chapter six .................................. 95
- How to sustain your influence ...... 95
  - Empower people ...................... 97
  - Stay connected ........................ 99
  - Do not step on toes .................. 100
  - Be humble ............................... 102
  - Persevere ................................ 104
  - Be selfless ............................... 105

Conclusion .................................. 108

Biography .................................... 121

# INTRODUCTION

The ability to positively impact people is an important skill for everyone. While enforcing your authority may work with people who work directly under you, it will not work for those who do not. On the other hand, influence will help you indirectly manage and control both those who work for you and those who do not.

Influence is an art that is in every aspect of life. Therefore, this book is relevant to you regardless of your vocation or the stage of your career—the principles for growing your influence are the same and apply to everyone. Regardless of what you do, you will need to influence peoples' actions and attitudes, at least sometimes.

Ideas, they say, rule the world. This is very true—but it is equally true, and even truer, that influence rules the world. Regardless of how great your idea is, it will not go far without influence. So, I can rightly say that "behind every successful idea is the right influence."

Without any doubt, it is good to have ideas, but it is also necessary to have influence. After all, what good is your idea if it could not affect the world the way that you want it to? Every person who has an idea, like you, wishes to see the idea become a positive reality.

It is a very frustrating experience when you see an idea that you have invested your time and resources in get little attention from your target audience. It is very painful for one's efforts to be wasted. No one invests in an idea to see it come to naught. This book was written to prevent this kind of frustration.

In short, this book is meant to show you how to influence people so that you can make your idea a home run. You do not have to force people to like your idea or do what you want— in fact, that is not a good way to market your idea! Instead, this book shows you exactly what you need to do to make your idea resonate with the right people.

Whether or not you believe it, everyone is business oriented. Everyone has something to sell. We sell all the time—we sell both tangible and intangible resources. The same principles apply to both kinds of resources.

Your ability to carry people along is directly proportional to how well you can influence them. Do you have people working under you? You need to understand the power of influence. Are you working under someone? You will need influence to rise to the top.

Do you have a great idea that you think will benefit the world? You will certainly need influence to get your idea heard. And if you want to be a natural and productive leader, you must learn the science of influencing.

I am happy to be offering you original tips on influence. In this book, you will not only learn how to influence people, but also how to influence situations—

though the difference is often very subtle. Sometimes, it is necessary to influence a situation, and other times, it is necessary to influence people.

I'm very confident that by the time you are done with this book, you will have learned how to influence your way to the top. I am also very certain that you will use this as your handbook for influencing people and situations.

# CHAPTER ONE

## Getting the right people on your side

This sounds obvious, but it still deserves emphasis. No matter how great your idea is, not everyone will be interested in it. Understanding this will make your work a lot easier and will save you from unnecessary pressure.

Get this: you do not have to influence everybody. Actually, you cannot influence everybody, so there is no need to waste time trying. Find the right people that will connect with your idea. Every successful company you see out there carefully considers demographics. Different products appeal to different genders. For example, more women than men are interested in cosmetics products. Some products are even more narrowly tailored. Some products appeal only to children, and these products are sold on TV programs that are solely targeted at children. If you are disinterested in a cartoon, but your child is captivated, the producer of that cartoon has accomplished their goal.

That TV show's producer has succeeded in influencing your child. When something resonates with you, it will have influence over you. For instance, a movie that has your attention will make you watch it until the end, and in the process, it will subtly alter your schedule.

You have now seen that influence lurks behind every decision. Whether we like it or not, we are influenced by something or someone all the time. You are perhaps reading this book because the very topic has influenced you to read it. The point is that something influenced you to read this book.

This is the power of influence. It is, therefore, very important to find the right people. The right people will easily connect with you; therefore, they will be easily influenced.

**Collaborate with like-minded people**

In a nutshell, I'm saying you need to find the right people to collaborate with. You cannot do everything by yourself. The last time I checked, no one could. Even the founders of big companies like Google and Facebook needed like-minded collaborators to reach the prominence they have today.

There is a popular maxim that "Rome was not built in a day." However, I need to add to this maxim. Rome was also not built by an individual. It was built by the collective efforts of many people. Influence feeds on influence. When you influence those you work with, they in turn will influence others. This is how influence works.

Alexander the Great had a very impressive leadership portfolio in the ancient world. By the time he was thirty, he had created one of the largest empires in the ancient world. He achieved this great feat because he was able to influence his generals, who in turn were able to influence the soldiers in their charge.

Alexander did not influence just anybody, but only like-minded people. He did not waste his efforts trying to convince peasants and cowards. He focused his attention on strong and brave people. Understand this: it is easier to influence those who believe in your vision than those who do not. Therefore, do your best to connect with like-minded people.

**Getting along with people**

Finding the right people is just the first step. I must emphasize, however, that it is more difficult to keep people's attention than it is to get it in the first places. It is one thing to find the right talented team; it is another to maintain them.

There are certain unspoken rules you must follow if you want to maintain your influence. I will be honest with you—influencing people is not cheap, and it is even less cheap to maintain your influence. There is work to do.

You must be able to get along with your workers, and people in general. In order to get along with people, you must do the following:

**Critique but do not criticize**

Though the two words *sound* quite similar—and some dictionaries even consider them to be synonyms—they are not exactly the same in application and meaning. *Criticizing* is finding fault in an idea, even if the idea's owner does not specifically request your input. *Critiquing* is carefully examining an idea in order to give an honest opinion about it, and it is usually requested by the idea's owner.

If you want to influence someone, the last thing you will want to do is to criticize their idea. Criticizing causes discouragement, which will eventually harm your ultimate goal of influencing the person who has the idea. Remember, you cannot work alone. If you could work alone, you would never need to employ that person or work with them.

Before you criticize the ideas of people, first consider the following:

1. They came up with the idea because they wanted to help.
2. They have spent their precious time in coming up with the idea.
3. They are already influenced by your own idea, and that is why they are coming up with something that will further promote your original idea.

Of course, give your critique when it is requested, and be polite and honest while giving it. Critique plays an important role in making progress. It is necessary to exchange feedback and ideas. However, criticism is never the solution. One can criticize from now until the end of time, and there still never be any improvement.

**Do not complain**

Even if you are not happy with something or someone, be diplomatic. This may not be easy to do, but no one says it is easy to have influence over others. You will only create a hostile working environment if you always express your dissatisfaction.

You cannot have influence by complaining. There are several ways you can make your opinions known without biting your tongue or frowning or tightening your jaw or clenching your fist or slamming the desk. You will end up weakening the chain of influence you already have if you are always complaining.

**Do not go about finding fault**

When fault-finding is the order of the day, productivity will inevitably be low. Fault-finding douses your workers' or teammates' enthusiasm and forces them to develop an unhealthy resistance to your attitude. This will greatly hamper your goal.

Intentionally commend and compliment your workers. There has to be something they are doing right that is praiseworthy. Publicly applaud them when they do something right and shelve your reservations for private moments. In other words, praise them publicly and correct them privately. You will be amazed at how fast and how much your influence will grow as a leader.

**Flexibility**

Great managers are flexible. They know when to correct and when to refrain. They know when to work alone and when to give room for others to contribute. You may be the boss, but you need to know when to listen.

In short, you must be willing to give way to others' influence. If an idea is better than yours, allow it to have its way. If you have to concede or accede, do. This is what flexibility is all about. Listening to others does not make you weak, nor does applying their opinions make you less influential or inferior. As a matter of fact, it is the exact opposite.

**Exercise self-control**

Self-control is undoubtedly the most important asset you could possess if you want to greatly influence people. A good manager and leader must be able to exercise self-control. If you cannot exercise self-control, you will find it extremely difficult to apply all what I have written so far in this book and all that I will treat in succeeding chapters.

The inability to exercise self-control has had negative impact on great managers. When your employees or teammates begin to question your decisions and policies, it is an indicator that your influence is already waning. In summary, you need to work with the right people to grow your influence, and you also need to have the right attitude to maintain your influence.

**THE EFFECTIVE ART OF INFLUENCE PEOPLE**

# CHAPTER TWO

## Effective communication

Communication is the act of exchanging information. In order to influence people to do a particular task, you will have to be sure you are effectively communicating. It is one thing to communicate, it is another to pass along relevant information. If you are not communicating clearly, there will be problems.

Communication is very important in any transaction. It is important for everyone who is involved in a project to be carried along from the outset. There is no room for assumptions or presumptions. You must not be presumptuous, and you must not be naïve.

One way to strike this vital balance is to communicate effectively. Leave no stone unturned. Take the time to communicate your mission and objectives. Break your project into milestones to make it easier for every team member to know exactly what you want.

By default, you have influence over those who understand you. This is because they will be influenced by your clarity to work towards achieving your goal. By contrast, if you do not communicate clearly, you lose your influence over others (when you have influence already) or fail to influence others when nobody understands your mission.

Asking questions is part of communication. A good communicator knows that he or she has been understood when his or her audience asks an intelligent question. When you give room for questions, you will know

## THE EFFECTIVE ART OF INFLUENCE PEOPLE

whether you have been understood or not, and you will know what to do to make them understand.

Also, do not be angry or frustrated when your team does not understand your points. If your anger is conspicuous, you will be channeling a negative energy that will dissipate your influence. It is hard to learn under duress; therefore, you must do your best to answer their questions in a relaxed manner.

The first step that you should take is to evaluate your presentation to see if the presentation is the problem or if they just do not get your idea. It's also possible that the project is beyond their professional knowhow, or it is just too difficult for them. If it is too difficult for them, try and simplify it. If they still do not understand, it is high time you changed your team. They may not be the right people for you.

You cannot honestly expect anyone to act on your instruction when they do not understand it in the first place. Effective communication is irreplaceable in project management.

To influence people, you have to communicate your message clearly; break down your project into smaller, relatable ideas; do not assume or presume—I repeat, never assume or presume; bring everyone along.

## Passion

Passion is contagious, and your passion is more likely to influence people than exerting force. If people cannot see your passion and zeal for your business or project, they may not be motivated. It takes passion to

## THE EFFECTIVE ART OF INFLUENCE PEOPLE

influence others to be as motivated as you are.

Passion is like fire; it consumes and spreads to every flammable object. Your passion for your project is what people are first going to connect with. It is also what will influence people to join your team.

When you have the passion, you can awaken peoples' desires to do what you want. The excitement, zest, and enthusiasm will be palpable, and your employees or team will naturally want to work with you and for you.

Also, passion arouses curiosity. People often act because they are curious. For instance, you are more likely to watch a movie that your friend is passionate about. His passion for the movie will arouse your curiosity, provoking a desire within you to watch the movie. When you eventually watch the movie, it will be because your friend's passion influenced you.

Can you see the power of passion? If you want to influence people to do what you want, you now know what to do: be passionate. Let people see your fervor and determination. Your passion will always ignite other peoples' passion.

## Listen twice, talk once

This is a figurative way of saying you should listen more and talk less. It is true that you are the owner of your idea; I am not disputing that. The entire project is yours—I get it. But if you want to have influence over your employees or teammates—or anyone for that matter—you must be willing to talk less and listen more.

The truth is that you cannot achieve your project alone. You need people to help you

## THE EFFECTIVE ART OF INFLUENCE PEOPLE

make it a reality. If you want to exercise a considerable influence over them, you must be willing to exercise patience as well.

Hear them out. Everyone has an idea. Do not do all of the talking all of the time. Be attentive to what they have to say, too. The only exception to this is if you are working with robots. However, whenever you are working with humans like yourself, you must be inclined to listen.

When they give you an idea, and you implement it, your reputation increases among them, and so does your influence. This is what many do not know. Some leaders wrongly assume that they will be seen as weak and stupid if they implement a subordinate's idea. However, this is wrong. When you implement a subordinate's idea, you improve your relationship and reputation with your subordinates. Your subordinates will also learn to trust and respect you—increasing the reach of your influence.

If you are looking for business partners, you must learn to stop talking about your business and yourself. Nobody wants to listen to your beautiful talk about your adventures and business acumen. No, that is definitely not how to grow influence. If anything, it is a great way to induce boredom.

You have to cultivate the habit of good listening. Allow other people to also talk about their ideas and plans. Hear what they want so that you will know how to come in. You must understand that it is not by the doing all the talking that you will be able to influence people.

Do you know that your silence can go a long way to influence the outcome of a discussion? There is an old African adage, "A fool is not known until he talks." When you allow others to speak first, you have an edge over them, because they do not know what is in your mind.

When your listener requests your input, he or she will naturally be inclined to attentively listen to all you have to say. This is your chance to influence the entire discussion. You will acknowledge all he or she has said so far and conclude with your own idea. This is another important way of influencing people.

## Be genuinely interested in others' point of view

People will know when you are faking it and they know when you are real. You must therefore be genuinely interested in peoples' opinions. When you allow people to freely express their ideas, they will also allow you to freely express yours.

For instance, if you are the coordinator for a project, you must be interested your team members' opinions. Let them know that they have your attention. Take your time explain the direction you want the project to take and what you want the end result to be.

Do not omit any relevant aspect. Remember, a well-understood project will be successfully executed. You must also let them know the scope and the limitation of the project. All this you must do to influence a good project.

You must also leave room for input. Be eager in entertaining questions and suggestions. You never can tell—someone might just provide the missing piece you need to successfully execute the project. A successfully implemented idea will boost

## THE EFFECTIVE ART OF INFLUENCE PEOPLE

your reputation. Of course, you know what that means for your influence.

Be alive during discussions and when you are brainstorming, so that you can correctly answer the questions; otherwise, they will know you are faking it and that will certainly hurt your reputation. Always answer their questions to the best of your ability.

As a matter of fact, demonstrate your interest in answering their questions. Encourage more questions. Their questions might call your attention to an ambiguous part of the project which may need some modifications. Your answers will also help them have a thorough understanding of the project. In the end, it will be a win-win for all parties.

Even if you are a member of the project team, you can still influence the discussion. By asking relevant questions and offering brilliant contributions, you are already influencing the coordinator of the project. Before you know it, the coordinator might make you his assistant or even put you in charge of an aspect of the project.

This influence comes, however, by paying attention to the project details. This is the only way you can understand the minutiae of the project, and therefore contribute brilliantly to the topic at hand. Regardless of whether you are the project coordinator or a team member, you can be an influence.

## Make your team feel important

Let every member of your team feel important. This is essential if you want to have influence over your team members. Let

## THE EFFECTIVE ART OF INFLUENCE PEOPLE

them know that you value them. In order to let them feel important and valued, you must do away with ambivalence. Do not run hot and cold.

High-productivity organizations all have one thing in common—they make their employees feel valued. They understand that the best way to control people is to satisfy them and make them comfortable. A satisfied employee will never have an excuse to be lazy or negligent.

Consequently, a valued employee will contribute maximally to his organization. Without even realizing it, the employee's attitude towards work is being influenced by his or her boss's kindness, creating a conducive working environment, and which is a motivating factor, together with the support of his or her boss.

Good human management's importance cannot be underestimated. You have to make your employees feel valued and comfortable. If you go the extra mile to make them feel valued and important, you can be sure they will also go the extra mile to please you. This is one of the secrets of successful companies.

Successful companies are successful because they pay handsomely and have other perks that come with the job. This does not mean that you should pay your employees beyond your budget to compete with these big companies; rather, what I'm saying is that you should take a cue from them and learn how to reward and compensate your workers.

This can include intangible forms of compensation. A simple "thank you" for a job well done will go a long way in making

## THE EFFECTIVE ART OF INFLUENCE PEOPLE

your employee feel valued. Public praising and commending a diligent worker is also a good idea. It's also a good idea to delegate your duties to your employees once in a while; this will also increase your influence among them.

While financial rewards can grow your influence, applying the above tips is often faster, always cheaper, and frequently more effective. Learn to appreciate people for their efforts and contributions to your cause. And if you are an employee, do your best to carry out your duties effectively; if you do this consequently, gradually, your reputation will grow.

# CHAPTER THREE

## Steer clear of arguments

The only person who will understand your idea is you. Therefore, you must be patient in conveying your idea to your team. Some people will get your idea immediately; others will not. There is nothing absurd about this. Everyone's comprehension ability differs, and that is all right.

It is also all right for people to disagree with your opinion. To this end, you must learn to accommodate people's opinions and at the same time learn to politely express your opinion. Your influence will not diminish if you entertain the ideas of others.

Authoritarianism does not guarantee your influence will grow. No doubt, you will succeed in creating fear in your employees,

## THE EFFECTIVE ART OF INFLUENCE PEOPLE

but that is that about it. When you disagree with an opinion, or someone disagrees with yours, be gentle and rational in settling it amicably.

Put sentiment aside; iron out the issue in a benevolent, mature manner. Understand that arguments will not solve the issue. Calm your nerves and re-explain your position. Listen to the other person's opinion. Make sure that you are communicating, not arguing.

Arguments can lead to quarrels, which will not help your cause. Always remember that arguing does not unite—it only divides. The only influence that emerges from division is negative. This book is all about positive influence, which is much more powerful. You cannot afford to allow disunity if you want to have a positive influence over people.

I am not suggesting that you should avoid engaging people in an intellectual discourse, where you explain your position and also listen; our point, however, is that you should never resort to heated debate about who is right and who is wrong.

Please, go ahead and prove your point, but do it politely and gently. You must allow the other person to also prove his or her point without interruption. Genuinely listen to his or her point of view so that you can truly understand his position.

The person who is trying to explain his or her point will appreciate your calmness and interest in wanting to understand him. At the end of the day, your maturity will be rewarded with an increase in your influence.

If you follow these steps, you may find yourself wondering how have you added to your influence. This is not farfetched. Your

**THE EFFECTIVE ART OF INFLUENCE PEOPLE**

patience in making your points known will be appreciated by the person; that maturity will lead to more respect and admiration. Thus, following this advice will lead to more and more influence. The person will hold you in high esteem. There you go!

## Apologize when you are wrong

You cannot be always right—that's impossible, and that is the plain truth. Everyone makes mistakes; even the best human is still a human. The most brilliant person in the world is still prone to errors. There is nothing we can do about this. It is part of the human package.

In the light of this, you will not always be right in your decisions and opinions because you do not know everything. So, admit it when you are wrong and apologize; apologizing will only earn your more respect. Refuse the temptation to be arrogant. Tendering an apology requires strength, so only the strong can do it.

One way to test your strength is to see if you can apologize when you are wrong. When you apologize, you are establishing your influence. Apologizing tells the offended person that you are reliable and humble. It also will indirectly influence them to hold you in high regard. Give this a try, and you will see how potent an apology is.

No man is an island. You cannot do everything all by yourself. You need people to help. This means that you will make mistakes, but this is not the problem. The problem is refusing to admit that you are wrong when you are wrong. When I last checked, tendering your apology will not remove a strand of hair from your head.

**THE EFFECTIVE ART OF INFLUENCE PEOPLE**

# Be gracious in your correction

Be gracious when correcting people when they are wrong. Your employees or team members can also be wrong for the same reason you also can be wrong. When this happens, refrain from categorically telling them that "they are wrong." Do not revel in their wrong, but lovingly correct them.

It is enough that they already know they are wrong; do not rub salt in their wounds by telling them how wrong they are. In addition, respect the fact that the reason that they are wrong is that they offered their opinions and ideas. If they kept their opinions to themselves, they would never be wrong.

One way to be gracious in your correction is to first appreciate their contribution. After all, they would never have offered their opinions if they did not have your interests at heart. You must consider this first before you correct them.

Furthermore, do not correct one person before others, unless the correction is collective. Correcting a team member privately will demonstrate that you are kind and understanding, and it will put you in the person's good books. As a consequence, your influence will reach another level.

Your team member may be wrong but learn to be generous in your rebuke. It is by this that you can grow and maintain your influence. By respecting others when you correct them, you will also be respected and looked upon favorably.

**Focus only on the present fault**

Make the fault or wrong easy to correct. Address only the fault of the moment—do

## THE EFFECTIVE ART OF INFLUENCE PEOPLE

not take the erring member or employee on a blame trip. Digging up the graves of past errors will create unnecessary animosity.

Be clear in your correction; let the person know exactly what he or she is being corrected for. Avoid tall tales and be precise. It is only by being precise on what the error is that you can influence the person to understand his or her error. In essence, in order to be influential, you must also be precise and articulate.

In fact, you are more likely to complicate the situation if you beat around the bush. By bringing up unrelated issues during the correction, the person you are correcting may end up more confused and frustrated.

### Show your fallibility

Be human in your correction. You have a higher chance of making an impact on the person you are correcting if you talk about a past mistake of your own—especially a related one—and describe how you rectified the mistake. Showing your fallibility also eases the burden of guilt on the person that you are correcting, and it also shows that you are relatable.

It is never a weakness to be vulnerable and be open about your mistakes. What some leaders and managers fail to realize is that claiming to be perfect has its own limitations. You will be creating an image you can never maintain to the end. One day, you will certainly make a mistake, to the utter dismay of those who have seen you as infallible.

When that day comes, people will be enormously disappointed in you. Why is this so? Because you have painted an untrue image of yourself. You are fallible like everyone else; it is therefore unnecessary to claim otherwise. It is better to play the fool and be seen as wise than to play being wise and be seen as fool.

## Vital questions to consider before correcting others

I will conclude this chapter by considering some essential questions that you should ask yourself before correcting people. You must bear in mind, though, that generally, the right way to correct the same way you would like to be corrected. Essentially, I'm suggesting that you put yourself in the shoes of the person you want to correct.

Ask the following questions before you correct:

**Is now the right time for correction?**

Timing is important in correction, just as it is important in everything. You may give someone the right advice, but if it is offered at a wrong time, it is good for nothing. Do not hastily correct. Observe the mood and the schedule of the person you want to correct. It is definitely a bad idea to correct a person that has just received bad news.

You also will not want to correct someone that has just been rebuked by another person. Doing so will cost you your influence. Though your aim is to correct their error, you will end up achieving something quite different. The last thing a frustrated person or a person having a bad day needs is to be reminded that he has made an error.

Save your advice until it is an opportune time, one when the person will be favorably disposed to your correction. You may go to

## THE EFFECTIVE ART OF INFLUENCE PEOPLE

the person when he is relaxed and calm. To be honest, there is no way that you can correct an angry person so that he or she will not find fault with your approach; there is also no way your correction will sink in when a person is confused or frustrated.

At the end of the day, you will have succeeded in making a new enemy or in wasting your time—or both. I have a feeling that you will not want to end up frustrated or make a new enemy for yourself; thus, I kindly advise that you correct someone who is wrong at the right time.

**Am I now in the right frame of mind to correct someone?**

It is not only important for the person you want to correct to be in the right frame of mind, it is equally important for you to also be in the right frame of mind. Logic tells us that positive energy will engender positivity, and vice versa.

This means that your correction will not go well if the person you want to correct is not in the right frame of mind, even if you are; it will also not go well if you are not in the right frame of mind, even if the person you want to correct is.

Hence, it is necessary for both of you to be in the right frame of mind. It will be very difficult to pass your message when you are angry. It is understandable that you are angry about your employee's mistake, especially if it is a silly one; nevertheless your anger will not solve the problem on the ground—if anything, it will worsen it.

Rather, what you should do in situations like this is to calm your nerves. You may say what you are not supposed to say when you are angry. It is therefore better to keep quiet

## THE EFFECTIVE ART OF INFLUENCE PEOPLE

until you are no longer angry. It is better to be safe than sorry; you will agree with us.

**Can this mistake be overlooked?**

I submit this to you that some errors are best taken with a grain of salt. You do not have to sweat or lose sleep over them. If a mistake does not in negatively affect you and it is inconsequential, please, overlook it.

Issuing corrections every now and then will not help your cause. Those who engage in a correction spree will not have the positive influence they deeply desire. If you want to have influence and to be reckoned with as a leader, you must learn to overlook some inconsequential errors.

If you are the type that always have something to correct and complain about, your effectiveness as a leader will be greatly reduced. Let your correction be rich and valuable. Be that person who everyone listens to when they correct. You will not be that person if you are always offering corrections.

When you learn to overlook some mistakes, you will be more greatly respected and valued. You will be treated like a lion, so that when you roar, your employees or team will know that something is truly wrong. Trust us, they will hold dearly all that you have to say. What better way is there to be influential than this?

**Is this a repeated mistake?**

Before you correct, you must evaluate if this mistake has been on your radar for a while or if it is a new one. Knowing whether an error is new or repetitive will help you know how to go about your correction. Tackling a stubborn error is obviously different from addressing a new error.

## THE EFFECTIVE ART OF INFLUENCE PEOPLE

It is unfair to be hard and harsh on your hard-working employee who has only made a mistake for the first time. If you do this, it will not go down well with that employee. He or she will feel unappreciated, and he or she may eventually be less motivated.

As your subordinate, he or she may not express his displeasure, but your bottle of influence has just been seared with a hot rod of inconsideration on your part. In order to avoid this ugly scenario, it is better to be kind in correcting this new mistake.

I will advise that you should be easy and casual with this person about the error. One way to do this is to bring the issue up in a conversation. Do not call that person specifically to rebuke him or her for that error. A simple expression like "oh, that reminds me…" is a good way to introduce your correction. This way, the employee will note the error and appreciate you for bringing it up lightly with him.

However, in the case of a repetitive error, you still do not have the prerogative to be hard or rude in your presentation, because that will not make the error go away. The best way to begin your correction is by asking the employee to explain the reason why he keeps repeating the same mistake.

This will give you the chance to see where the problem lies. It may be a misunderstanding on the part of the employee, or it may be that you are the one giving them the wrong signal or message. It may also be that the job scope is beyond the expertise of the employee.

Whatever the reason may be, what matters is that you now know it. You will then take the appropriate steps, and the issue will be solved one way or the other. Whatever your

## THE EFFECTIVE ART OF INFLUENCE PEOPLE

decision is, there is high probability that the employee in question will accept the outcome, because you have taken genuine interest in understanding the root cause of the error.

Congratulations, you have just added another feather to your cap in your pursuit of influence.

# CHAPTER FOUR

## How to sell your ideas

So far, in this book, I have shown how you can influence people in different ways. In this chapter, however, our focus will be on how to sell your ideas. Recall that I stated in the *Introduction* that influence rules the world.

Influence rules the world in the sense that it is through influence that ideas are sold. Your idea may be both groundbreaking and breathtaking, but if it does not reach the right people, it is useless. In other words, the success of your idea is contingent on how influential you are.

It is good to have ideas, but it is better to know how to sell your ideas. Every successful idea owner understands the

## THE EFFECTIVE ART OF INFLUENCE PEOPLE

power of influence in marketing ideas. You also need to have the charisma to market your idea to people.

Your idea is only as good as your influence. Nobody cares whether your idea is promising or not. What is the point of having an idea nobody knows about? I will stop speaking in parables and hit the nail on the head: your idea is worthless until it is paid for.[2]

With the proliferation of information—courtesy of the revolution in the technological world—it is becoming an uphill battle to sell your ideas, because there are many ideas on the internet. The competition is getting fiercer by the seconds. What do you do? Do you fold your arms and watch as others try to use influence to get their way, or do you face the competition head-on?

In the remainder of this chapter, I will be looking at different ways you can influence people to buying into your idea. I can assure you that once you religiously and patiently implement these tips, your ideas will appeal to the right people.

**Identify your market**

As seemingly obvious as this sounds, many sellers do not know their market. If you do not know your market, your idea is bound to fail woefully. The first thing you should do is to identify the market for your idea.

As a matter of fact, your market should guide you in molding your idea. You should know your buyers from the outset; otherwise, you will have a hard time making sales, because you will be attempting to influence the wrong people.

## THE EFFECTIVE ART OF INFLUENCE PEOPLE

The plain truth is that your idea is not for everyone, because it will not benefit everyone; it will not interest everyone. Hence, it is your duty to identify your market from the very beginning. Your chance to influence people to buy your idea is much better when they are interested in your idea.

For instance, an idea that will revolutionize the entertainment industry may be not be suitable for the technology industry. You must do research to nail your market. Beta test your idea with your friends and family and encourage them to give you feedback, so that you will know how to make your idea better and more relevant. The suggestions and critiques you receive from your beta users will help improve your idea. In the end, your idea will sell better because of its appeal.

## Brand yourself

After identifying your market, the work has only just begun. You also need to brand yourself. Your personality is the first thing people will notice, before you even have the chance to sell your idea. Therefore, you must brand yourself and create an appealing image. Your personality can greatly enhance or detract from your influence; a lot depends on how you carry yourself.

If you do not look convincing about your idea, you will be betraying your idea. Let your carriage and demeanor be charming. If you get this right, chances are you will have already influenced your target to buy your idea.

Personality is very important in influencing sales. Big companies know this, and this is why they make celebrities the face of their products. They do this to influence their

## THE EFFECTIVE ART OF INFLUENCE PEOPLE

sales. While good sellers know that not everyone is interested in their products, they also know that many will be interested in the face of their product.

You also need to take your branding to the social media. In fact, this is the best way to brand yourself. Companies are now on social media. They get more followers and more customers. Their followers are comprised of both their original customers and the fans of the celebrities that these companies use as their ambassadors. If they play their cards right, it is the latter group of followers that will eventually turn to customers. It is all about influencing sales for you.

Let us be frank with ourselves, people are not always interested in the product. There are many things that influence consumers' decisions to buy products; personal branding is one factor. Alongside the product, people also buy charms, charisma, confidence, knowledge, passion etc.

Your personality can influence people into buying your idea. First impressions truly matter when it comes to selling your idea. Your knowledge of your idea, your passion for your idea, and your confidence in your idea all come to play in influencing your buyers.

Understand this: ideas are often similar, but individuals are not. There is something unique about everyone. You must therefore leverage your personality, since chances are you are not the only one with that idea, and there are also countless ideas that are similar to yours. However, your personality will make you stand out if it is used well.

This is why you must take personal branding very seriously. It exerts a great influence on

## THE EFFECTIVE ART OF INFLUENCE PEOPLE

people's perception of your product. Your personality will always influence people either negatively or positively. On the one hand, people may buy your idea because of your personality, but on the other hand, they may reject your idea because of your personality.

The reality is that people will always have a perception of you, and it is your responsibility to influence your buyers to have a positive perception about you by investing in better branding. This will take us to the next step for selling your idea.

### Know your competitors

While you should not intrude into your neighbor's privacy, it is a good idea to "peep" through the window to look at the activities of your competitors. In the business world, peeping is allowed.

Before you can peep at what your competitors are doing, you will have to know who your competitors are. A reputable sales man once warned that "business is a battlefield,"[3] and he is right. If a soldier does not know who his enemies are on the battlefield, he is as good as dead.

Similarly, if you do not know who your competitors are, you will not know what they are up to, and that translates into losing out in the market. It is of utmost importance to know the competitors in your niche, if you want to influence the market in your favor.

By knowing your competitors, you will also be able to see what they are doing to influence the market, and what they are not doing well. You can then use this knowledge to market your own idea. You will know

## THE EFFECTIVE ART OF INFLUENCE PEOPLE

what pitfalls to avoid and what strategies to implement.

If you want to be influential in your niche, you must be ready to do some foundational work. Find out who is selling what, how they are selling it, and who they are selling it to. Observe their selling techniques and see if there are any that will benefit you.

It would also help you if move towards their buyers. Now that you have come to know your competitors' buyers, it is time to say hello to them. There is a saying, "the enemy of your enemy is your friend." It is also applicable to your buyers— "the buyer of your competitor is also your buyer."

Never forget this. If they can buy from your competitor, then they can also buy from you. I will now go to the next step on how to influence people.

**Build your army**

You have worked on your idea and you think it is now ready to go and bless lives. As the *general* of your product's army, you will need soldiers that will fight for your idea and gain ground. At this point, I believe you have come to know your market and that you have identified your buyers and learned where you can meet them.

This is the information age, where you can sell your idea to millions online. With just a click, you can communicate your ideas to many people at once. To be clear, however, you do not want communicate your idea to everybody; you only want to put it before your buyers.

**Digital marketing**

The easiest way to go about this is, like I have stated earlier, is to identify your

## THE EFFECTIVE ART OF INFLUENCE PEOPLE

competitors' buyers. Social media has made it very easy to do this—all you need to do is to perform a key word search that is related to your idea, and you will see thousands of people who are also interested in what you are doing.

You can even find competitors in your area by searching by location, using filters and hashtags. In fact, I advise you to focus on local competitors. Find out who their followers are and engage with them.

Managing social media is serious work, but it is worth it. In order to get the attention of your competitors' followers, you will have to also drop reasonable and intelligent comments in the comment section of your competitors' posts. This is your chance to announce yourself; do not drop arbitrary or trite messages like "nice" or "cool." Instead, state what is nice and cool about the post.

Give a carefully constructed comment that will command people's attention. Leave an intelligent message that will compel followers and competitors to visit your profile and follow you.

This is how you can build your reputation and announce your presence on social media. Do not shy away from using relevant hashtags that will make people find you. Never ignore comments on your posts; make sure you reply to all comments—unless they are in hundreds.

Randomly visit your followers' pages once in a while and like their posts or leave a comment. Before you know it, you will be a great influence to reckon with in your niche. Similarly, apply these tips to brands that will be interested in your idea. Because social media is not the aim of the book, I will stop

## THE EFFECTIVE ART OF INFLUENCE PEOPLE

here with how to be influential on social media.

It would also be great to have a blog or a website where you can direct your followers to buy your products. Though this requires hard work, it is a proven way to sell your ideas. You will find out that sellers that have blogs or websites effectively reach out to more people than those who do not.

**Analogue marketing**

Analogue marketing still has a very place important in marketing. Focusing only on digital influence is like putting all one's eggs in one basket. If you want to be a force to reckon with in your niche, you have to use both digital and analogue tools.

They are not mutually exclusive—your online connection can lead to physical connection and your physical connection can lead to online networking. The more people you meet in person, the better it is for your online presence. You can always refer people to your social medial profiles.

The techniques used in analogue marketing are quite different from those used in digital marketing, but the principles and virtues are the same. Networking with people outside of social media will require you to leave the comfort of your home.

First, you need to find the location of these companies around you. Asking people or a simple search on your favorite search engine will let you know the addresses of the established companies who are likely to buy your idea.

Also, use the opportunity to acquaint yourself with information about these companies. This will help you to narrow down your list of potential companies to the

## THE EFFECTIVE ART OF INFLUENCE PEOPLE

ones where your chances for success are higher. In essence, I'm suggesting that you make a priority list. Put the companies you are most interested in at the top of your list.

At this point, we would like to remind you why we are telling you to do all these things: they are necessary to place you on a higher pedestal, so that you are able to influence your product and idea sales. Now that you have your priority list ready, it is now time to start making strategic pitches.

**Strategic pitching**

At this point, it is necessary for you to make intentional efforts to sell your ideas to people that matter. Now, you need to engage with executives of the companies that you are interested in and acquaint them with your idea. You will have to make your pitch pithy. Get straight to the point; there is no time to beat around the bush.

Do not tell them your life story, or how you have suffered and toiled to make ends meet. That is desperation, and it does not sell. Desperation will turn your buyers off. Rather, tell them what this idea can do for them. Let them know how it will help their company grow bigger and better.

This is how you can sell your idea. This is how you can influence sales. Your confidence and your ability to show them how this idea will boost their company is what will get your idea sold. Make your entire pitch about them.

It is really important to understand how your idea will help your buyers before you pitch them. One way to do this is to put your idea in the form of a well-written proposal. Try to wait for a week after submitting your

# THE EFFECTIVE ART OF INFLUENCE PEOPLE

proposal before you contact your potential buyer again.

If you still have not heard from your potential buyer, after a month, move to another buyer. Or, better yet, you can pitch two or more buyers at the same time. There is nothing wrong with that—you will have the opportunity to go with the highest bidder, and your chances of getting a buyer will also be higher.

## Be an expert: creatively demonstrate your idea

Every seller wants a buyer. If wishes were horses, beggars would ride. Unfortunately, beggars do not ride because wishes are not horses. This is the reality of the world we live in. Beggars will have to work hard if they want to ride.

This simply means that anyone who wants to be successful must work hard. To sell an idea, you must have solid knowledge about that idea. If you want to make people say "yes" to your idea, then you must be an expert.

Spend time on your idea; keep getting better and better with it. After all, what is worth knowing is worth knowing well. Study hard and extensively on your idea. Ask questions from those who have more experience than our in your field. To be an expert, you have to mingle with experts. That is how it works.

If you do not have the privilege to meet these experts for a têtê-à-têtê, you can get their scholarly works and books. As you can see, you will spend your money, but the investment will be worth it at the end of the day.

## THE EFFECTIVE ART OF INFLUENCE PEOPLE

The more knowledge you have about your idea, the better you will be at demonstrating it in different creative ways. A teacher who is very sound in a subject will be able to teach that subject using different examples.

When your buyers see how knowledgeable you are about your idea, they will definitely want to become your clients, because you have illustrated it in many ways they can understand. Your knowledge has influenced their decision to buy your product.

Therefore, if you want to influence people, you must have the knowledge that they do not have. Ignorance has always kowtowed to knowledge. The world favors those with knowledge. This is why wisdom is better than power.

What wisdom can do, power may not be able to do, but wisdom can do all that power can do. I therefore advise you to invest in wisdom, and power will become your servant. I cannot emphasize this cardinal truth enough. Your knowledge will give you an edge above others, allowing you to affect their decisions.

People will always want to buy what they connect with. Ask yourself, will you also want to buy a product that does not strike a chord with you? Of course not. Your ability to make your product strike a chord with your buyer is directly proportional to your knowledge about your idea and your buyer.

That is to say, your knowledge about your buyer will help you to properly channel your idea to meet their needs. It is by knowing a company's void that you can fill it. Herein is the logic. For example, if you have an idea on how to accurately monitor the number of

## THE EFFECTIVE ART OF INFLUENCE PEOPLE

eggs produced in a large poultry farm, you must address this issue in your pitching.

You have to let the farm manager know that you understand the problem they are facing and how your idea can solve the problem. Break your points down in a way he will understand; show him that you know what you are talking about, and he will have no choice but to buy your idea.

You have to make him connect with your idea on a personal level before he drops the cash. The reason he will give you the job is because you make him buy into your idea. If you want to influence your sales, you must be able connect with your buyers at the point of their needs.

Be genuinely concerned about their problems—or at least make them believe that you are. It is normal for buyers to be skeptical about a product, especially if it is a new one; therefore, allow them to reiterate their challenges to you. Even if you have understood what the problem is, still generously allow them to express themselves.

When you do this, you are indirectly communicating that you really care about their concerns. However, if you cut them short while they are expressing themselves to you, you communicating the wrong message about your personality. Your buyers will think you are only after their money and that you are not interested in their problem. This assumption will negatively influence their decision, and they may end up not buying your idea. At the end of the discussion, they will tell you that they are not interested, or if they are polite, they will you that they will call you when they

## THE EFFECTIVE ART OF INFLUENCE PEOPLE

need your help. Believe me, that is never going to happen.

It takes patience and kindness to influence sales. You are the one that wants to sell; you must therefore be willing to exercise patience and answer a plethora of questions. Anyone who tells you that it is very easy to sell ideas is deceiving you. It has never been easy, let alone in this competitive age.

Selling your idea is not easy. If it were, you would not be reading this book. However, I'm very confident that if you apply all that you have learned from this book, you will have an edge over many sellers. That we can assure you.

# CHAPTER FIVE

## The science of being influential

According to Merriam-Webster Dictionary, science is the state of knowing knowledge, as distinguished from ignorance or misunderstanding. Therefore, the science of being influential is the understanding of the operation of laws guiding influence, especially as obtained and tested through scientific method.

In essence, what I am driving at is that influencing people is a science of its own. That is to say, there are laws to follow if anyone wants to be influential. Nobody is influential overnight. Building your influence is like building your reputation. It takes time before people know you for something.

## THE EFFECTIVE ART OF INFLUENCE PEOPLE

In the same vein, if you want to let people know you as a person of influence in your field, you have to follow some principles and laws.

### Cause and effect

For every cause, there is an effect. This means that you cannot leave things to chance. This is a general principle of life, and it is applicable to being influential. This principle can also be called the principle of sowing and reaping.

Farmers understand this very well. No farmer will sow nothing and expect to reap something. Also, no farmer will sow bananas and expect to reap apples. If you want to influence people, you must think like a farmer.

Ask yourself, what seed of influence have you sown that you are expecting to reap?

Have you done your part before you expecting others to do theirs? The idea you want to sell—have you given it your best? The project that you have built a team to execute, do you really understand it?

Are you yourself doing what you want others to do for you? Are you working hard? If you are a parent, are you leading by example for your child? Are you exhibiting qualities of a good leader? If the answers to these questions are not in the affirmative, then you will not reap positive influence. In fact, you should not expect to reap any.

Doing your part will influence others to do theirs. Your rich knowledge about your idea will have a positive influence on your buyer. Your firm knowledge about the project at hand will help you influence people at work.

If you want people to do something for you, show them how to go about it by doing it. If

## THE EFFECTIVE ART OF INFLUENCE PEOPLE

you want your team to be transparent and honest, show them with your actions. If you want your buyer to buy your product, show them how your idea is working for you. If they are not sure your product is working for you, they may not want to buy.

If you are not up and working like a leader, you will not earn the respect you deserve; consequently, you may not be that much of an influence in decision making. If you are a parent, the best way to influence your child is by doing what you want him or her to do and avoiding what you do not want him or her to do.

You will do things differently if you always remember that you will reap what you sow. The mirror will reveal who you are. You will make the bed that you will lie on. The principle of cause and effect is a vital principle to remember if you want to be influential.

**Value**

The principle of value is another important principle to understand. Values are the backbone of success. Big businesses like Microsoft and Apple are successful because they have high-value propositions.

Put differently, when you buy from these companies, you get more in value than you exchange for your money.[4] If what you are offering is of great value, you do not have to say much to convince someone to buy it.

Be fair with your product's price. Do not overinflate the price. This will turn your people off. At the same time, you should also not underprice your product or idea. This is a sign of desperation and it is not

## THE EFFECTIVE ART OF INFLUENCE PEOPLE

going to help your influence; on the contrary, it is going to harm it.

For instance, drastically reducing your rate in order to land the job will do more harm than good. Clients can easily identify a rate that is based on desperation. Clients know the range of a standard rate—even terrible clients who are notorious for going for the lowest bidder knows this.

The first thing to note is that reducing the value of your service is never a good way to land a job. The best way you can influence your client's decision is to submit a good proposal—one that is pithy and perfect.

If you do want to reduce your rate, do not make it lower than the lowest standard rate, because the client will judge you by your rate. A low rate suggests to the client that you are either desperate or inexperienced.

Your rate also must not be very high—unless you have the experience and the wherewithal to execute the project you are bidding for. It will be laughable and ridiculous if your rate is high and your proposal is trash. The client will easily find out whether you have the experience or not.

All in all, be fair in your appraisal of your service's value. Make sure you give your best in delivering the job. The best work is the best influence, not the cheapest rate. Take time to work on your proposal—address the client's challenges, propose clear solutions, and the job will be yours.

**Attraction**

The law of attraction may sound overtly philosophical, but it works. How you see yourself is how others will see you. You will be addressed the way you are dressed. When

## THE EFFECTIVE ART OF INFLUENCE PEOPLE

you respect yourself, people will also respect you. These are proven facts of life.

If you want others to be confident in yourself and your ability, you first have to be confident in yourself and what you can do. Confidence is attractive. When you reek of confidence—even if you are not very good at that thing—you will be more convincing.

Still, as the law of attraction teaches, if you cannot see yourself competing at top level, you will find it difficult getting to the top. Your mind is the battle ground; it is the pot in which your thoughts and aspirations are cooked.

What you feed your mind with is what will guide your conduct. This is why people are encouraged to read. "Readers are leaders," they say. You cannot get to where you cannot see—it is impossible. Hence, the saying that, you attract what you believe.

If you are a salesperson, and you do not see yourself selling, that will remove your motivation to sell. It is when you see yourself selling that you will be motivated to sell. If you are negative about your business or yourself, you will be seeing negativity all around you.

By contrast, a positive attitude will keep you inspired and energetic. It will help you to be mentally fit. Never forget the law of attraction—you have to see yourself influencing people if you are serious about influencing people.

**Sacrifice**

To sacrifice is to give away something that is valuable in order to gain something else of value. In the game of chess, sometimes, it is

## THE EFFECTIVE ART OF INFLUENCE PEOPLE

wise to sacrifice some pieces to expose your rival's king. This is wisdom, and you will need to apply it to your quest to becoming influential.

There are some habits you have to give up if you want to be a person of influence. You cannot afford to live like those without vision. You will have to be up and working. This means you will have to sacrifice long hours of sleep. You will also have to sacrifice binge watching. In a nutshell, you must be ready to sacrifice your comfort.

The people of great influence that you see today sacrificed a lot to be where they are now. They did not become influential by sleeping and watching movies. They gave up pleasure and comfort to be who and what they are now.

If you want to be a leading voice in your field, be prepared to embrace rejection and denial. You also have to be patient and humble. Influence grows gradually; it does not spring up overnight. Like a tender plant, it requires a lot of care and attention. It has to be watered with patience, hard work, and consistence.

Do not be discouraged if you think your influence is not growing at the pace you expect it to. Look into why its growth is stunted; if it is something you are not doing right, correct it, but if it is natural, give it some time. Keep working and hoping for the best. Never give up.

**Integrity**

You should never build your influence at the expense of your reputation. The saying, "a good name is better than riches" is an eternal

# THE EFFECTIVE ART OF INFLUENCE PEOPLE

truth. Of what use is your influence if it is built upon a shady and shaky foundation?

Warren Buffet said it all in his wise quote, "it takes 20 years to build a reputation and five minutes to ruin it." This is very true! You may build your influence for donkey's years, but it only takes a moment to vitiate it.

The question then is: why build your reputation on lies and questionable methods? Instead, you should build your reputation by following ethical principles, like the ones I have stated in this book. Truly, it takes diligence and consistence to build reputation, but it is worth it.

The temptation to use underhanded techniques to build your reputation will be there, but do not yield. Prioritize quality over quantity. It is better to start small and end big than start big and end small.

**Time**

Everything has its own time. There is a time for sowing and a time for harvesting. Understanding this will save you from many headaches. The failure to understand time has led many to make wrong moves and incur loses.

When it is time for sowing, do not expect to harvest. As obvious as this sounds, many people go about their businesses expecting to reap during sowing season. Your sowing season is the time to work hard and make some headway.

It is the formative age of your idea. If you get it wrong at this stage, every other thing will go wrong. Therefore, you have to put in your best work here. You should not do the

## THE EFFECTIVE ART OF INFLUENCE PEOPLE

right thing at the wrong time, and you should not do the wrong thing at the right time. Timing is of great importance.

If you get it right at this stage, your harvest season will certainly come. You will have to be patient and keep working. The more you keep working on your idea, the better you will become, and the more influential you will also become. You will naturally get good at what you do often.

In addition, you must work with time. Time waits for no one—it does not even wait for you to check where the minute hand and the second hand are. What this teaches you is that you should also be time conscious.

Do not procrastinate. You cannot afford to delay a task that is integral to your project. Procrastination has caused many people to lose their jobs, money, projects, and influence. You do not want to experience this.

Promise yourself a nice treat if you beat a deadline. This is one way to overcome procrastination. You can also break your project into milestones that you can finish in no time. If you work aimlessly, you will not be productive. Always set a target for yourself that you must meet in a given time. This will help you to be time conscious and productive.

In summary, be a good time manager. Create schedules to follow and religiously follow your schedules. One of the qualities of successful people is that they have excellent time management. They are judicious in their use of time.

**THE EFFECTIVE ART OF INFLUENCE PEOPLE**

# CHAPTER SIX

## How to sustain your influence

I am concluding with this topic because I am confident that you will become influential. Consider this chapter to be a bonus from us. Sustaining influence is just as herculean a task as growing influence. Do not for a second assume that you can relax now that your influence has grown.

(Do not forget, I'm assuming that you have applied all the tips I have suggested in this book, and you are now very influential in your field; this means that you can now easily influence people. Therefore, this chapter is for those who already have influence.)

If you ever harbored the idea that getting to the top is the natural end of hard work, please drop the idea. It is not true. I'm not scaring you; I'm only being sincere with you. People at the top work twice as hard as those who are not, because more is at stake.

Africa's richest man, Aliko Dangote, told Bloomberg in an interview, "I'm surprised I'm getting even four hours of sleep a day. I'm going ahead full steam." If someone in the upper echelons of management is sleeping less, what is your excuse?

If a tremendously successful business tycoon, a multibillionaire (in US dollars) is saying he and his team are going full steam, What does that tell you? That you have work to do! That you cannot afford to let your guard down. That you cannot give in to sleep and complacency. That you have to keep working to sustain your influence.

The ones who call the shots at the top have a lifestyle that looks a lot like Dangote. They

## THE EFFECTIVE ART OF INFLUENCE PEOPLE

are always working. They are great time managers. The greater their influence, the more the work. I must warn you that a life of influence is not a life of mediocrity.

Hence, if you believe that you can get to the top and stop working, I'm sorry to inform you that it does not work this way. You cannot have your cake and eat it. That is to say, you cannot crave influence and not work. In this chapter, I will teach you what you must do to sustain your influence and top level.

**Empower people**

If you want to remain influential, you have to empower and invest in people. Investing in people is like sowing seeds, which will grow into trees that will in turn grow many branches. These branches are connections.

Nobody has it all, and nobody knows it all. Whether you like it or not, you will always need people's input from time to time. Even world leaders need people to work with.
You can easily contact the people you have empowered to help you execute your tasks.

They will gladly help you out, because you have helped them. You can empower people by helping them to get jobs, by helping them to establish their businesses, by employing them, by imparting knowledge into them, etc.

For instance, if you need help with a company, you can always contact the person that you helped to secure a job in that company. Those you have established in their businesses will always be there to assist you in any way they can. Those you have taught skills to will gladly use the same skills to help you when the need arises.

# THE EFFECTIVE ART OF INFLUENCE PEOPLE

Those whose educations you have sponsored their education will definitely be of help to you someday. This is how you can sustain influence in this ever-competitive word. The more people you empower, the more influence you will have.

## Stay connected

I will tell you this truth: there is no such person who ever gets to a stage where he no longer needs others. There is no such person! Rich people keep getting richer because of connections. Governments keep forming coalitions because of the need to sustain their power and relevance.

Companies and individuals collaborate to have a formidable influence in their niche. The reasons for these collaborations is either to rekindle a dying influence or to further reinforce a steady influence. This is a preemptive strategy to stay relevant.

If government and big companies are working this hard to sustain their relevance, then you should go even further to sustain your influence. The god of influence favors only those who are working hard to sustain their influence.

As much as you are able, keep your connection with people. Keep your friendships. Contact your friends, workers, and acquaintances once in a while. Attend seminars and conferences and make new friends. The key is to do everything legal and ethical to keep your connections.

**Do not step on toes**

People who live in glass houses should not throw stones. This wise proverb is all the more pertinent to those who are already at

## THE EFFECTIVE ART OF INFLUENCE PEOPLE

the top of their game. It is easy for those at the top to come crashing down. A person that is already down will not worry about falling.

This means that you should avoid stepping on toes. Do not cut corners or cheat your way to the top. If you do that, you will provoke those that are below you to work for and look forward to your downfall. They will do all they can to bring you down. They really do not have anything to lose, but you do.

In the same vein, do not engage in unhealthy competition with your rivals. Be civil and respectful in your dealings with them. You never know when you might need their help. They may be your rivals, but they are also influential in their own way. Never underestimate them.

When you keep in your own lane, you will not step on toes, and there will not be any problem. This is one of the secrets of successful companies. I'm not saying you should not compete with your rivals. Please do, it is good. I am saying, however, that you should engage in a healthy competition.

**Be humble**

Be humble. Always remember the days of your humble beginnings. Appreciate everyone who has helped you to be where you are today. Pride will cause your downfall. You should never be arrogant or condescending to your workers—or anybody else, for that matter.

Make yourself approachable. It is only when you are approachable that you will be able to know everything that is happening around you. Arrogance will cost you vital information that you should know. But if

## THE EFFECTIVE ART OF INFLUENCE PEOPLE

you are approachable, people will find it easy to come to you and keep you abreast of new developments.

Give orders politely. Nobody is disputing that you are the leader, and humanly giving orders will not invalidate your leadership. Address people by their names; do not call people by whistling or tapping. Calling them by their names will make them appreciate you more.

Honestly appreciate people when they do something for you. Let them know you are very grateful. This will make them do more next time. You should apply this same principle to your employees. Commend those who are hard workers and appreciate them.

Workers who are appreciated will be more productive and mentally fit than those who are not. This is not rocket science. It is a principle of life. The law of reciprocation says you get what you give. Therefore, when you appreciate people, they will also appreciate you.

**Persevere**

The fact that you are at the top does not mean you do not need to persevere. The road of success is unpredictable. Things will not go the way I have planned all the time. Tragedy may hit, and losses may be incurred. Nonetheless, in all of this, you must persevere.

You have to be strong. Do not make impulsive decisions that will harm your reputation. You may be tempted to do it but do not cave in. The way to success is an endless journey. No one has all the successes in the world. There will always be needs to meet and tasks to complete.

## THE EFFECTIVE ART OF INFLUENCE PEOPLE

You must therefore steadfastly persist in pursuing success. Come rain, come shine, you must never stop pursuing your goals. Keep working. Keep going. Keep being positive.

**Be selfless**

In your busy schedule, remember to help others in whatever way you can. Pay attention to your team members, your employees, and those around you. When you see that they are sad or unusually quiet, ask them what the problem is.

Everything must not be about work. Show genuine concern and help them solve their problems in any way you can. This will go a long way towards building your influence. People will note your selflessness and help you when the need arises.

Selfishness does not induce or sustain influence. On the contrary, it extinguishes whatever flames of influence you have left. Many assume that their influence will grow when they focus only on themselves—but this is a very wrong. You will easily influence people when you are selfless.

Consider this example. Let's say that you approach Mr. A to help you out on a problem, and he goes through a painstaking process to help you. On another occasion, you approach Mr. B to help you solve a problem, but he refuses to help you, citing the risk involved as the reason for his refusal.

Who will you help when the need arises? Of course, it is Mr. A, who goes through risk to help you out. What influences your decision to help him? His selflessness. You may also help Mr. B, but you will first help Mr. A.

## THE EFFECTIVE ART OF INFLUENCE PEOPLE

And if the two of them come at the same time, it is obvious who you will help: Mr. A. Hence, the fulfillment of the proverb, "one good turn deserves another." Selflessness always pays.

# CONCLUSION

Influence is all about exerting an effect on someone or something. It is the capacity to effect a change on someone's opinions and actions. In other words, influence is the ability to provoke a reaction or response, either directly or indirectly.

A person of influence is a powerful person, because that person will have the power to effect the desired change in any given situation and even on people. An influential person will be able to affect people's decisions.

Influence is an art, and it is those who understand it that can make people do what they want. There are principles you have to follow if you want to bend people's sentiments and situations to your idea. This

## THE EFFECTIVE ART OF INFLUENCE PEOPLE

book has been written to show you what these principles are.

Good communication is very important in influencing others. You have to be clear and unambiguous in stating what you want. Do not leave the person you want to influence guessing. A wrong message may lead to a negative effect on your influence.

Poor communication or incomplete messages can lead to an end result you do not wish for. It is therefore very important to be very clear and articulate when disseminating information. People will always be influenced by your communication and your actions.

Thus, you must be careful not to communicate the wrong message with your actions. Do away with ambivalence, for it can wrongly influence someone to do something you do not desire. This is what wrong influence is. If you want something done, be clear about it.

If, at the same time, you do not want something, be vocal about it. Your decisiveness will help the person know your position on the issue. The fact is, whether it is clear or ambiguous, your position will influence others. Accordingly, it is better to be vocal about your position on things.

I have emphasized the importance of working with the right people earlier in this book. It is a bad idea to think that you can influence everyone all the time. Trying to influence the wrong people may backfire, and even have a negative effect on your influence.

Human management skills are also required if you want to influence people. I have generously listed several ways of managing

## THE EFFECTIVE ART OF INFLUENCE PEOPLE

human resources. Your humane characteristics will go a long way in affecting how those around you respond to you.

People will naturally respond to you when they see how genuinely concerned you are about their welfare and challenges. They are also more likely to respond to your request or situation when you call for it. Your humaneness and kindness is the cause of this influence; therefore, never stop being kind.

Do your best to always get along with people. Do not see anyone as irrelevant and useless. In reality, no one is irrelevant or useless. The worthless person in a team may later be the sole savior in certain unpredictable situations.

The person that is poverty-stricken today may be the one that will help you tomorrow.

Your subordinate now may end up becoming your superior tomorrow. These are the realities of life. To that end, you owe it yourself to treat everybody with respect and decency.

Everyone that you come across feels important—especially those who you work with. Be kind to strangers; help the less privileged; give to the poor; help your friends; treat your subordinates with kindness. This is how influence is built. It is not by stampeding on everyone's toe or ridiculing the very existential essence of people.

I reiterate again the importance knowledge in influencing people. If you want to influence people, you need to have the knowledge they do not have. Read more extensively on subjects related to your field

## THE EFFECTIVE ART OF INFLUENCE PEOPLE

and make sure to gain more general knowledge.

Make reading a lifestyle. Listen to news to keep yourself abreast of local, national, and international developments. Always remember that the most knowledgeable person is the most powerful person. Knowledge can overcome power, but power cannot overcome knowledge.

Therefore, rather than focusing on might and brutality, invest in wisdom. The person that deals with people with wisdom will have a more lasting influence than the person that deals with people with power. People are bound to keep quiet and listen to you when you know something they do not now.

However, people can challenge you, even with your power, when they know something, especially more than you do.

Can you now see that wisdom is a greater influence than power? Do not settle for less or for any mediocrity. Keep on adding to your knowledge if you want to be influential.

Your ability chance to influence people will be limited if you are only interested in you. I'm not saying you should not talk about your interests or your ideas, but you should also be keenly interested in the interests of other people, too.

Give people the chance to talk about their interests and ideas. When you give them this opportunity, they will be influenced to listen to your idea as well. For example, as a counselor, you have a higher chance of making someone talk if you begin your conversation with their interests.

Do your homework: find out what interests them and what topics you should totally

## THE EFFECTIVE ART OF INFLUENCE PEOPLE

avoid. Assumptions will not work; rather, they will have a negative impact on your conversation. If you are not sure about the person's interests, it is better to ask the person directly or ask those who will know, like friends and family.

In this book, I also devoted an entire chapter to marketing your ideas. There are certain things you must do in order to be a successful seller. First, you must concurrently work on your idea and identify your market. Let the two be mutually inclusive—work on your idea with the potential buyers and consumers in mind.

This will help you to effectively tailor your idea to better suit the tastes of your buyers. This requires that you understand your buyer's challenges. Your work is to make your idea suitable for solving their challenges. When you do this, you have a better chance of selling your idea.

While you are working on your idea, do not forget to brand yourself. Carve out a special kind of recognition for yourself. In other words, make it easy for people to identify you and your product. You can do this by creating a unique logo and color theme for your brand. Be consistent in using this theme.

Take advantage of social media. Do not wait until you finish your idea before you create your social media. Keep your followers updated on what you are doing and where you are. Accompany your posts with appropriate high-quality pictures and relevant hashtags.

However, be careful about what you post on social media. Do not reveal too much at once. It is not all the time that you should

## THE EFFECTIVE ART OF INFLUENCE PEOPLE

post about your idea. You can post topics you think your followers will appreciate.

You should also ask questions. Posts with questions usually have high engagements than post without picture. Send your heartfelt wishes during festive periods and holidays. However, avoid polarizing topics that are political or religious. This can negatively impact your influence.

As you do all this, you will be increasing your social media reach. Inform your followers beforehand when your idea will be available for sale. You should also take advantage of adverts by promoting your posts to reach a larger audience. You will sell more this way.

In addition, you should know your competitors so that you can learn from them. You will always see what you are doing wrong and what you need to improve on. You will also know what you can do to make your idea unique.

The way to sustain your influence is to keep doing what makes you influential in the first place. Keep doing all you did to become influential. When you refuse to add logs to a campfire, it will die out. No matter how fiery a fire is—even if it is an inferno—it will stop burning the moment there is nothing to burn.

Similarly, your influence will begin to die the moment you stop feeding it with the principles and qualities you used in building it. Staying at the top level requires hard work and consistence. You have to be passionate to stay at the top of your game. It is only passion that can keep you going when you are down and discouraged.

## THE EFFECTIVE ART OF INFLUENCE PEOPLE

Do not let money or other perks be the only source of your motivation, because there will be times when the money and perks will not come. But your passion will keep you on your toes when the road becomes muddy and slippery.

I'm glad that you read this book to the end. I also congratulate you because you will soon have testimonies. Be rest assured that your influence will grow significantly if you apply all the principles you have learned from this book. I cannot wait to hear your success story.

# BIOGRAPHY

Raphael Dume, is an American author, researcher, serial entrepreneur, and investor. His work has been found to improve self-esteem, resilience, happiness, optimism, and curiosity, while reducing symptoms of depression, anxiety, and anger.

He focuses on helping others by documenting his personal learning and experiences through his writings. He hopes to share his work that are easy to understand and strategies that can be easily applied in everyone's day to day life.

He continually works on expanding his knowledge by reading, attending seminars, taking courses, and networking with other professionals.

He is currently lives in New Jersey with his family.

www.ingramcontent.com/pod-product-compliance
Lightning Source LLC
Chambersburg PA
CBHW022010170526
45157CB00003B/1213